Plague and Pandemic Alert!

Julie Karner

Crabtree Publishing Company
www.crabtreebooks.com

presented by:

Crabtree Publishing Company

www.crabtreebooks.com

To all of the brilliant and dedicated scientists who spend their days crusading against modern plagues.

Coordinating editor: Ellen Rodger

Book design and production coordinator: Rosie Gowsell

Cover design: Rob MacGregor

Photo research: Allison Napier

Copyediting and indexing: Wendy Scavuzzo

Scanning technician: Arlene Arch-Wilson

Consultant: Eric M. Maiese, MHS, Johns Hopkins University, Bloomberg School of Public Health, Department of Epidemiology

Photographs: AP/Wide World Photos: p. 21 (bottom), p. 22 (bottom), p. 25 (top), p. 26 (bottom), p. 28 (top); Archives Charmet: p. 4; George Bernard/ Photo Researchers, Inc.: p. 12 (top), p. 13 (top); Bettmann/Corbis/Magma: p. 3, p. 16 (bottom), p. 20; CDC: p. 12 (top left), p.19 (middle); CDC/ Jim Gathany: p.17 (bottom); CDC/ Dr. George Kubica: p. 15 (top); CDC/Dr. Mae Melvin: p. 16 (top); CDC/ Dr. Pratt: p. 12 (top right); CDC/Science Source/Photo Researchers, Inc.: p. 16 (middle); Jean-Loup Charmet/Photo Researchers, Inc.: p. 12 (bottom); CNRI/Science Photo Library: p. 6 (top); Dick Clintsman/Corbis/Magma: p. 23 (bottom); Howard Davies/Corbis/Magma: p. 19 (bottom); Jim Dowdalls/Photo Researchers, Inc.: p. 21 (top); Eye of Science/Photo Researchers, Inc.: p. 26 (top); Dr. Cecil H. Fox/Photo Researchers, Inc.: p. 14 (top left); Giacomo Pirozzi: p. 18; Gideon Mendel/Corbis/Magma: p. 22 (top); Louise Gubb/Corbis/Magma: p. 14 (middle), p. 29 (bottom); Jean Francois Hellio & Nicholas Van Ingen/Photo Researcher, Inc.: p. 13 (bottom); Hulton Archive by Getty Images: p. 25 (bottom); S. Kaufmann & J. Golecki/Photo Researchers, Inc.: title page; Laurent/Lesache/Photo Researchers, Inc.: p. 10 (top); Dr. Kari Lounatmaa/Science Photo Library: p. 10 (bottom); Mary Evans Picture Library: p. 24; Minnesota Historical Society/Corbis/Magma: p. 15 (bottom); North Wind/ North Wind Picture Archives: p. 23 (top); Dr. Steve Patterson/Photo Researchers, Inc.: p. 11 (top); Caroline Penn: p. 19 (top); Photo Researchers, Inc.: p. 28 (bottom); St. Bartholomew's Hospital/ Photo Researchers, Inc.: p. 5; Science Source/Photo Researchers, Inc.: p. 6 (bottom), p. 27 (bottom); Peter Skinner/Photo Researchers, Inc.: p. 7 (top); Dr. Linda Stannard, UCT/Photo Researchers, Inc.: p. 16 (middle); Underwood & Underwood/ Corbis/Magma: p. 17 (top); VVG/Science Photo Library: p. 7 (bottom); Hamish Wilson: p. 27 (top)

Illustrations: Roman Goforth: p. 9; Dan Pressman: p. 8; David Wysotski, Allure Illustrations: pp. 30-31

Cover: Children in an Indonesian elementary school wear masks in Jakarta, Indonesia, in April, 2003, to prevent the spread of the deadly flu-like Severe Acute Respiratory Syndrome (SARS).

Contents: People line up for smallpox vaccinations outside Morrisania Hospital in the Bronx, New York City, in 1947. The fear of an outbreak that had already killed two people made city politicians and doctors advise people to get vaccinations.

Title page: A colored electron-microscope image shows a battleground not visible to the human eye. The bacteria that causes tuberculosis is shown in green. The yellow-colored cell is a macrophage that fights foreign bacteria such as the TB bacteria.

Crabtree Publishing Company

www.crabtreebooks.com   1-800-387-7650

Cataloging-in-Publication data

Karner, Julie, 1976-
  Plague and pandemic alert! : disaster alert! / written by Julie Karner.
    p. cm.
  Includes index.
  ISBN 0-7787-1580-9 (rlb) -- ISBN 0-7787-1612-0 (pbk)
  1. Epidemics--Juvenile literature. I. Title.
  RA653.5.K375 2005
  614.4--dc22

                                    2004013085
                                         LC

Published in the United States
PMB 16A
350 Fifth Ave.
Suite 3308
New York, NY
10118

Published in Canada
616 Welland Ave.,
St. Catharines,
Ontario, Canada
L2M 5V6

Published in the United Kingdom
73 Lime Walk
Headington
Oxford
OX3 7AD
United Kingdom

Published in Australia
386 Mt. Alexander Rd.,
Ascot Vale (Melbourne)
V1C 3032

Table of Contents

Plagues of Terror

A plague is a deadly disease that spreads easily among people. Hundreds of years ago, people blamed plagues on nature, the gods, and the arrangement of the stars and planets. People were terrified of plagues because there seemed to be no way to stop them. Today, we know plagues are infections caused by viruses and bacteria, and that the diseases they bring do not always kill.

What is a disaster? A disaster is a destructive event that affects the natural world and human communities. Some disasters are predictable and others occur without warning. Coping successfully with a disaster depends on a community's preparation.

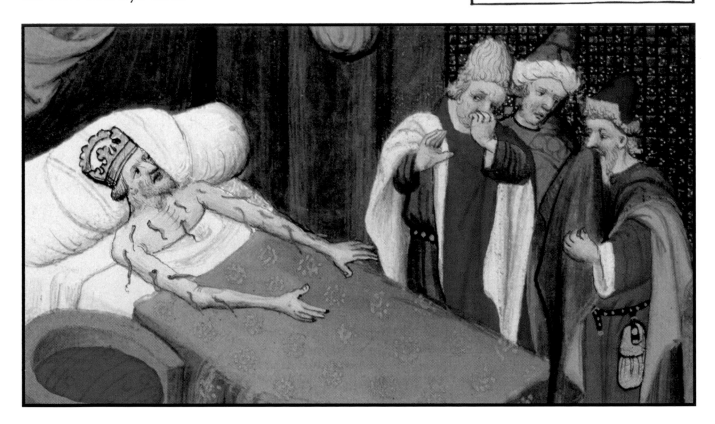

The word plague describes a **devastating** and widespread **infectious disease**. Throughout history, wherever humans have gathered in settlements, plague has followed. Thousands of years ago humans roamed large sections of land, hunting and gathering their food. Very few people died of plagues then. It was more difficult for disease to spread because people lived far apart.

(above) Plague is used to describe a number of diseases today. It originally referred to one particular disease: the bubonic plague, or the Black Death. Early doctors used leeches to suck the blood out of plague patients.

Spreading disease

When humans began to farm and settle permanently in one location, infectious diseases became more common. In cities and villages, people lived closer together and shared food and water. People also lived close to where they threw their garbage and toilet waste. Where waste collected, germs and germ-spreading pests, such as rats, had the perfect environment in which to grow and spread disease.

Plague myths

Plagues made people fearful because they did not understand them. They made up stories to explain the cause of a disease and to make it less mysterious. In Germany and Scandinavia, the Black Death was thought to be caused by a plague maiden who sailed through the sky at night, scattering plague poison in her outstretched hand. People also believed "foul air" such as fogs and mists caused plagues. To ward off the plague and purify the air of evil smells, people burned incense and carried flowers. Some "cures" for the plague included cutting open and draining sores, burning sores with hot pokers, and applying dried toads to draw out evil toxins. Some people actually bathed in, or drank goat urine, believing that it would drive disease out of the blood.

In the Middle Ages, a period of time from 500 A.D. to 1500 A.D. in Europe, plague doctors tended the sick. Doctors wore long robes and cloth coverings shaped like beaks over their heads. It was thought that the beaked hats prevented the spread of the plague to the doctors.

The Science of Plagues

Scientists have learned a great deal about plagues since the days of using dried toads as medicine. We now know that disease begins with a single germ and can infect one person or millions of people.

Epidemics and pandemics

Diseases that always exist in a population are called endemic diseases. Colds, the flu, and chickenpox are examples of endemic diseases. An epidemic happens when a disease infects more than the usual number of victims and spreads quickly. When an epidemic becomes so widespread that it affects a large geographic area, such as an entire country or continent, it is called a pandemic. Human Immunodeficiency Virus, or HIV, the virus that causes AIDS, or Acquired Immune Deficiency Syndrome, has become a pandemic, affecting more than 40 million people worldwide.

What causes plague?

It was once thought that sickness was a punishment for bad behavior. A scientific explanation of the cause of disease, known as germ theory, was developed by two scientists, Louis Pasteur and Robert Koch, during the 1800s. Germ theory explained that each disease is caused by a different microscopic organism called a germ.

(top) The virus that causes chickenpox is made visible under an electron microscope.

(bottom) Scientist Louis Pasteur discovered that disease could be caused by bacteria that was passed from person to person.

Most contagious diseases are caused by tiny life forms, or microorganisms such as bacteria and viruses. Bacteria are so small they can only be seen through a **microscope**. Bacteria are everywhere! Some bacteria are harmless and live in soil, water, and even on our skin and in our mouths. Pathogenic, or disease causing, bacteria cause an **infection** when they enter the body. Infection occurs when microorganisms multiply in a person's body.

Viruses are smaller than bacteria. They are so small they can only be seen with a special microscope called an electron microscope. Each virus has a different shape and appearance which makes it identifiable under the electron microscope. In order to multiply, a virus must infect a **host** animal or plant on which it lives. It is difficult for a virus to live outside of a host.

(right) The electron microscope is so powerful it is used to identify the tiniest viruses.

(bottom) The human tongue is home to hundreds of bacteria. Most of them are harmless, or good bacteria that help the body fight off bad bacteria.

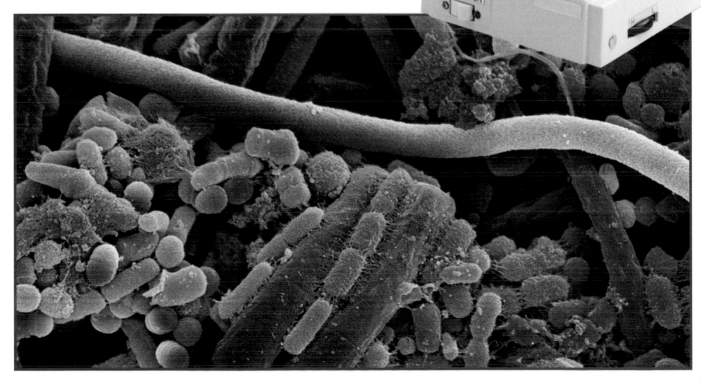

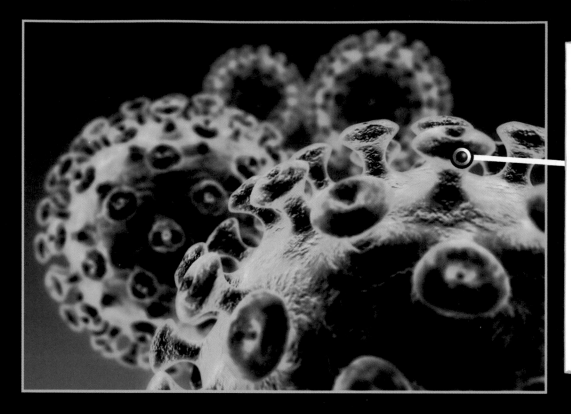

A microscopic view of the HIV virus. Viral knobs or proteins allow the virus to attach to cells. Inside the virus are chemicals that allow the virus to create a reaction and multiply in a host's body.

War is declared!

The human body fights battles everyday with microorganisms, or **microbes**. In most of these battles, the body's defense system fights back and the body remains healthy. When microbes are able to overcome the body's defenses, disease develops.

Infections

Once a microorganism enters the bloodstream, the body's **immune system** goes to work. The body recognizes intruders or microbes that are not normally found in the bloodstream. Special **white blood cells** called phagocytes and macrophages, gather around a site where bacteria have infected a **tissue** and begin to attack the foreign cells. Eventually, the bacteria are swallowed up by these white blood cells. The phagocytes and macrophages are war heroes of a sort: they die in the process of defending the body against outside invaders. The **pus** that

forms in scrapes and scratches is partly made up of these dead white blood cells filled with the dead bacteria they have digested. Phagocytes and macrophages are not the only defense the body has against infection. Every invading microbe either produces or has on its surface **molecules** that are recognized by the body's immune system. These molecules are called **antigens**. The body then produces **antibodies** to fight the intruders. If the same disease attacks the body again, those antibodies are ready and waiting to sound an alarm call. The faster the invading microbe is recognized by the body, the more likely the immune system will be successful in destroying it.

Infection and disease occur when the immune system cannot kill off all of the invaders. The bacteria or virus multiplies within the tissue and can be carried by the bloodstream, spreading it to the rest of the body.

The immune system

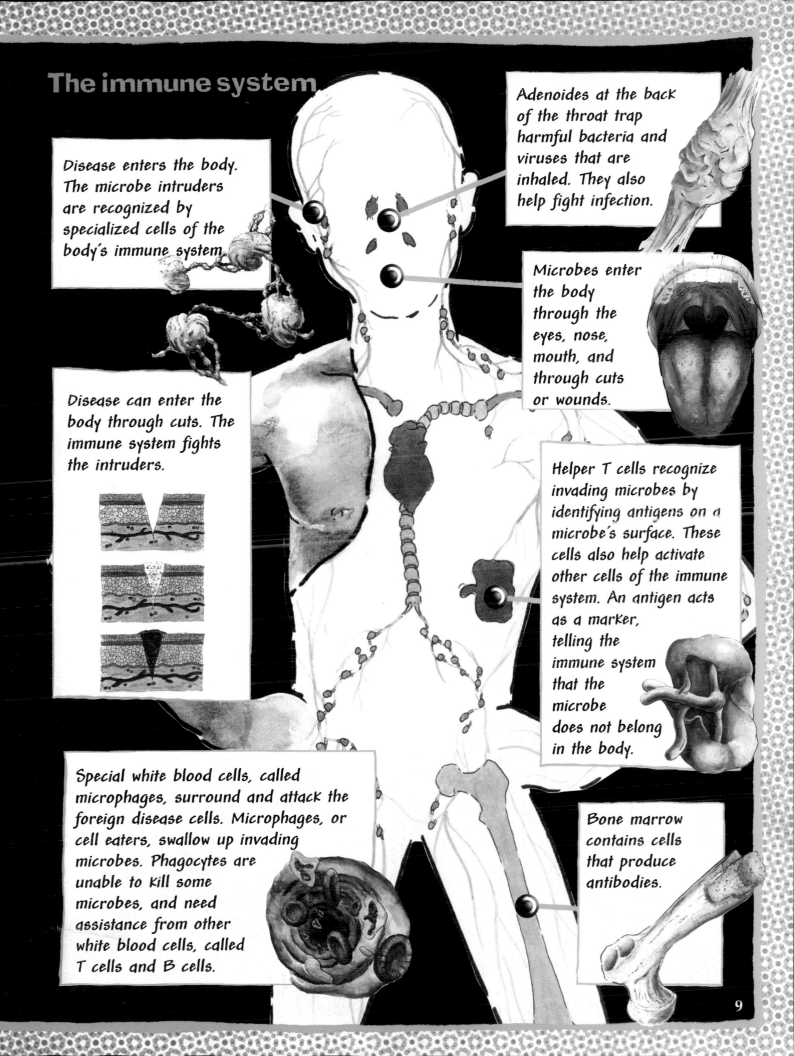

Disease enters the body. The microbe intruders are recognized by specialized cells of the body's immune system.

Adenoides at the back of the throat trap harmful bacteria and viruses that are inhaled. They also help fight infection.

Microbes enter the body through the eyes, nose, mouth, and through cuts or wounds.

Disease can enter the body through cuts. The immune system fights the intruders.

Helper T cells recognize invading microbes by identifying antigens on a microbe's surface. These cells also help activate other cells of the immune system. An antigen acts as a marker, telling the immune system that the microbe does not belong in the body.

Special white blood cells, called microphages, surround and attack the foreign disease cells. Microphages, or cell eaters, swallow up invading microbes. Phagocytes are unable to kill some microbes, and need assistance from other white blood cells, called T cells and B cells.

Bone marrow contains cells that produce antibodies.

The Life of a Plague

A plague begins with a single disease microbe that reproduces to form an army of microbes attacking a single person. The disease spreads when microbes are passed from person to person.

Disease-causing microorganisms enter the body in a number of ways: by breathing them in as dust or tiny droplets in the air, through food and liquids that contain disease microbes, or through the bite of an infected animal or insect. People may also become infected if they touch a surface covered with disease microbes then touch their eyes or mouths, or if the microbes enter a wound on the body. Some diseases pass from person to person through bodily fluids such as saliva or blood.

Some common disease symptoms include coughing, sneezing, aches, and nausea.

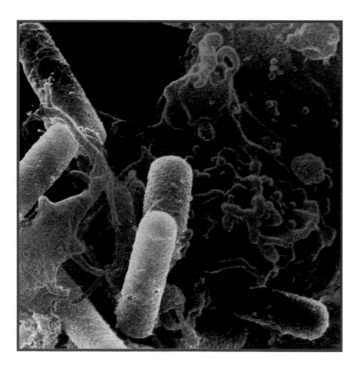

Part of the body's immune system, white blood cells (shown in orange) attack disease bacteria (shown in blue).

Great place to live

The body is an ideal home for bacteria and viruses to grow, if they can overcome the immune system. The immune system attacks disease. Redness and fever are two signs that the immune system is fighting disease. Redness results from blood being directed to the infection site. Fever is caused by the body's white blood cells fighting the infection, and producing heat. These physical signs are called symptoms. Symptoms are signs that the body is fighting a disease, but sometimes the body becomes so weak from this battle that it cannot recover.

 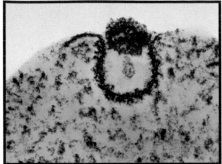 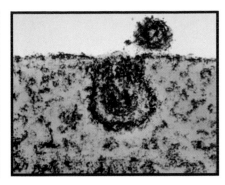

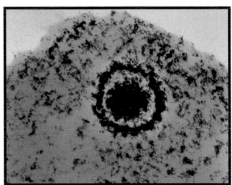 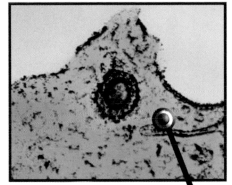 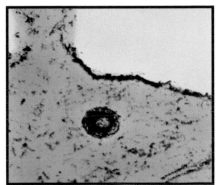

Virus attack

A virus or bacterium uses energy from its host, the human body, to grow and divide. It may also produce poisons in the body. If the invading microbes are allowed to grow in the body without being killed by the immune system, they eventually use up so much energy that they kill the person with the disease.

Death is not the end

The death of the host, or person carrying the disease, does not always mean the end of the disease. Some bacteria, such as Bacillus anthracis, that causes the disease anthrax, can produce cells called spores. When these spores are not actively growing or dividing, they lie in a sleep-like state for many years until they find another host. When a sheep, cow, or human breathes in these spores, the spores become active and the disease bacteria reproduces, or multiplies.

Anthrax spores are breathed in by humans and animals, such as this sheep. The disease itself does not become active until the spores are breathed in.

Catching the flu
These six images show the flu, or influenza virus, infecting a person through the nose or mouth. The flu virus is round with a spiky outer shell that allows the virus to attach to host cells, that appear watery and blue. The virus penetrates the host, infects it, and causes more influenza viruses to be produced.

The life of the bubonic plague

The bubonic plague began its attack on Asian fleas and rats. It traveled all the way to Europe, where it infected and killed millions of people. The bubonic plague was caused by a bacterium called Yersinia pestis, that is found in rat fleas and their usual victim, the black rat. Rat fleas also bite humans. During the Middle Ages, changes in **climate** and the way people lived brought humans in closer contact with rats. This gave the rat flea and the plague bacteria a greater chance to feed on humans.

The bubonic plague was so frightening that many people abandoned relatives to be cared for by religious orders. The plague killed 25 million Europeans between 1347 and 1351.

When a flea bites a host, either rat or human, it transfers blood into the bite wound, passing on the plague bacteria. The bacteria then multiplies in the host's blood. Plague-carrying fleas lived on rats. Rats lived close to humans during the Middle Ages and the fleas often bit humans as well as rats.

Pus and fever

Symptoms of the bubonic plague in humans included high fever, vomiting, and egg-sized swellings filled with pus, called buboes. Buboes formed on the neck and in the armpits and groin. Dark reddish-black spots or rings also formed from bleeding under the skin. Most victims died within three to six days of being bitten by a flea. The Black Death was also caught through coughing or sneezing. This very contagious form of the bubonic plague was called the pneumonic plague. People with pneumonic plague had difficulty breathing and suffered bouts of coughing. They often died within hours of being infected.

The plague spreads

Over several years during the Middle Ages, the Black Death spread from Asia across Europe. Today, a person can board an airplane and travel around the world in a day. As a result, disease spreads more quickly. The Black Death began to claim victims in China in 1333. In 1347, the plague hit Western Europe. In those days, the average person rarely traveled far outside their own city or town. People walked wherever they were going, or they rode on horseback or in mule-drawn carts. Long journeys were made mostly by traders and **religious pilgrims**. These people brought the plague from Asia to Europe, infecting people in towns along their way. Many graves of pilgrims dating from 1338 to 1339 have been found along trade routes between Asia and Europe.

The Bills of Mortality is a list written during the 1665 plague of London, England. It lists all of the 68,596 deaths that occurred in that year from bubonic plague.

Locusts

A plague of locusts refers not to a disease, but to millions of hungry insects. Locusts are a type of grasshopper that fly in swarms. They eat everything in their path, including grains and tree leaves.

Desert locusts swarm in Africa. Locusts are a plague because they completely destroy crops.

Famous Plagues

Diseases are as numerous as the bacteria and viruses that cause them. Humans have battled many different diseases over the past several thousand years. Some of these diseases are common today only in third world countries, where poor sanitation systems allow disease to spread rapidly.

A modern-day plague

Acquired Immune Deficiency Syndrome (AIDS) was first identified in 1981. It is a disease that weakens the immune system's T cells, making victims unable to fight off infection from other diseases. AIDS is now a pandemic that has killed millions. AIDS is caused by the Human Immunodeficiency Virus (HIV), that is transmitted from person to person in bodily fluids. The disease is especially deadly in countries where poor people cannot afford the AIDS drugs that will keep them alive. So many people have died of the disease that in some African countries, orphanages are filled with children whose parents and other relatives have died.

Everyday, 14,000 people worldwide are infected with HIV, the virus that causes AIDS. That is a rate of almost ten people per minute. Three million people died from AIDS last year, including the person (above) whose coffin is being taken for burial in Botswana.

Tuberculosis

Tuberculosis, also known as consumption or the white death, kills two million people each year. TB, as tuberculosis is called, is a disease that has survived for thousands of years. Tuberculosis is transferred from person to person on tiny droplets of saliva or mucus propelled into the air by coughing, sneezing, or talking. These droplets are breathed into the lungs, where the body's immune system battles the bacteria they carry.

Tuberculosis infections can scar the lungs and cause victims to cough up blood. It can also spread to other parts of the body, carving holes in the bones of the arms, legs, and spine. In the mid-1800s, people with TB were sent to hospitals called sanitoriums. Fresh air and rest were believed to help patients recover, so most sanitoriums were located in forests or mountains. Medical scientists developed a drug to treat tuberculosis in the 1940s.

Children infected with tuberculosis rest in their beds at a Minnesota state sanitorium in 1915. Tuberculosis was often fatal until the 1940s when scientists developed drugs called antibiotics that fought tuberculosis bacteria. As patients were treated with drugs and cured, sanitoriums closed. Today, tuberculosis is once again infecting people because the disease microbes have developed a resistance to the drugs.

Malaria

Malaria has killed more people over the course of human history than any other disease. In fact, it has killed more people than any war or famine. Each year, it infects 300 million people and kills at least one million. Malaria symptoms include fever, chills, and sweating. It is caused by the parasite Plasmodium that is transferred from person to person by a mosquito bite.

Yellow fever

Yellow fever is also spread through the bite of a mosquito, but it is caused by a virus. Yellow fever gets its name from one of its common symptoms: jaundice, which is a yellowing of the eyes and skin caused when liver cells are attacked by the virus. British hospitals during the 1800s separated yellow fever sufferers from other patients. They dressed them in jackets covered with yellow patches to mark them as contagious. This led to fever victims being called yellow jackets. Today, yellow fever infects 200,000 people per year and causes 30,000 deaths.

West Nile virus

West Nile virus was first discovered in 1937, but the first case of a human being infected by the disease in North America was not until 1999. Mosquitoes spread the disease. Most people who get the virus suffer from headaches, stiff necks, fever, and skin rashes. In some cases, the disease can cause death from swelling of the brain. The virus killed 284 people in the United States in 2002.

An epidemic of yellow fever in New Orleans, Louisiana, in the 1800s, killed hundreds of people. Cities and towns located close to swampy water often had epidemics of mosquito-spread diseases such as yellow fever and malaria before medical scientists developed drugs to fight the diseases.

Spanish flu

The Spanish influenza killed so many people from 1918 to 1919, that funerals were shortened and carpenters had trouble making enough coffins. The flu was reported in Spain at the end of World War I and spread around the world within two years. It is estimated that 20 to 40 million people died from the disease. Many died within hours of contracting the virus. They suffered head and body aches, sore throat, and often **suffocated** when their lungs filled with fluid. The influenza eventually waned, but scientists today are still studying the 1918 virus to know more about why it was so deadly. They also want to know how to prevent future flu outbreaks from becoming deadly pandemics.

The Spanish flu pandemic killed millions and made others fear for their lives. Even baseball players and fans in the stands refused to attend games without protective face masks.

Mosquitoes' revenge

A mosquito bite is never very pleasant, but sometimes it can actually be deadly. While the bubonic plague was spread by rats and fleas, some diseases, such as malaria, West Nile virus, and yellow fever are spread by mosquitoes.

Female mosquitoes spread disease from victim to victim when puncturing human skin on their quest for blood. The blood is used to nourish their developing eggs. After the mosquito sucks up infected blood from one person, the parasites multiply inside the mosquito. The insect then passes the disease on to its own offspring or injects parasites into the next person it bites.

Plague Warriors

The human body does an amazing job of fighting off disease, but plagues would be far more common if not for the efforts of doctors and scientists. These experts not only treat the disease, but they also study its cause and try to prevent it from becoming an epidemic.

The microscope

It was once thought that illness was caused by "bad air." Some early scientists even suggested that disease might be caused by invisible living things, but no one could find proof of this idea. It was not until scientist Antony van Leeuwenhoek used light and two pieces of glass to magnify a small sample of liquid that these invisible living things became real. Looking through his simple microscope, van Leeuwenhoek saw tiny living beings that he called animalcules. These creatures would later be called bacteria and protozoa. The use of the microscope has made it possible to identify an organism that causes a particular disease.

Disease diagnosis

When people are sick, they usually go to a doctor to find out what is wrong with them. The doctor takes the patient's temperature to see if there is a fever. The doctor will also ask what symptoms the patient is suffering from. Sometimes it is not possible to tell what disease a person has just by the symptoms. The doctor then takes blood samples to send to a laboratory, or lab, to identify the disease.

A laboratory worker examines blood samples under a microscope to identify the disease a patient has. Researchers examine blood, urine, tissue, and saliva samples. Each disease has a different "pattern" visible under the microscope.

Plague doctors

A special group of scientists, called epidemiologists, follow the spread of epidemic diseases. They try to find out the cause of a disease, how it is spread, and where it is likely to occur. The more they know about a disease, the more they can do to fight its spread. If the spread of a disease is stopped early, an epidemic can be avoided. Doctors and scientists in hospitals, universities, and private companies around the world work hard in the fight against disease. They study diseases, and make medicines to treat and prevent them. Researchers also educate people about disease prevention.

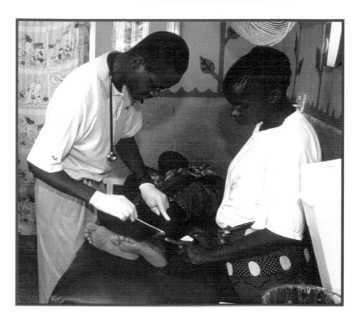

(top right) A doctor examines a patient in a malaria hospital in Kenya.

(right) Field researchers in protective equipment work at the site of an Ebola outbreak. Ebola is a deadly virus that causes fevers and bleeding inside the body.

A group of women and children in Orissa, India, attend a malaria prevention workshop. The workshop gives the women information on how to avoid places where mosquitoes breed and protect themselves from being bitten. They also learn the symptoms of the disease and possible treatments.

World Health Organization

Some diseases are so destructive that they require the co-operation of governments all over the world in order to stop them. In 1948, the **United Nations** developed a special **agency** to deal with the health of people around the world. The agency, called the World Health Organization (WHO), represents 192 countries and tries to reduce the spread of disease. The Centers for Disease Control and Prevention (CDC) in Atlanta, Georgia, perform a similar role in the United States. National organizations throughout the world, such as Health Canada, Communicable Diseases Australia, the National Institute of Infectious Diseases in Japan, and the National Disease Surveillance Centre in Ireland all work to watch, prevent, and control the spread of plagues and diseases. These organizations have laboratories that study disease microbes, and how the diseases they create affect people. The disease-prevention organizations also develop plans to fight pandemics.

Needling away disease

Mumps was once a very contagious virus that affected mostly children. People with mumps look like chipmunks because the disease causes swelling in the salivary glands between the ear and jaw. Sometimes, the disease caused deafness or even death. It was just one of many common illnesses that are now controlled by immunization. When people are immunized, or vaccinated, it means they are protected against a disease. Children in the United States and Canada are now vaccinated against mumps when they are babies.

A little boy suffering from the mumps wears a bandage on his head. Scientists developed a vaccine for mumps in the 1960s.

Stopping the spread of SARS

Severe Acute Respiratory Syndrome (SARS) first appeared in late 2002 in southern China. The disease, caused by a virus, has symptoms including high fever, headache, cough, and difficulty breathing. It is thought to be spread by droplets of saliva or **phlegm** coughed or sneezed into the air. Teams of experts from the WHO followed the disease's trail, from the first reported victims to each new case worldwide. Warnings were issued about international travel, and travelers were asked to stay away from SARS-infected areas. For each person diagnosed with SARS, doctors tried to make a list of all of the people that patient had come in close contact with since catching the disease. These people were then quarantined, or kept out of contact with people who had not been exposed to the disease until doctors could be certain that they were not infected. The SARS outbreak was declared officially over only when no new cases appeared in 20 days, or twice as long as it took for the disease to develop in new victims.

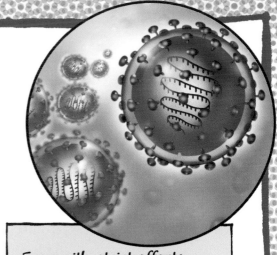

Even with strict efforts to control SARS, 8,098 people were infected and 774 people died over several months during 2002 to 2003. Hospital workers and visitors had to wear face masks and caps. Hospital visits were limited because nobody wanted the disease to spread. The disease made people fearful and careful.

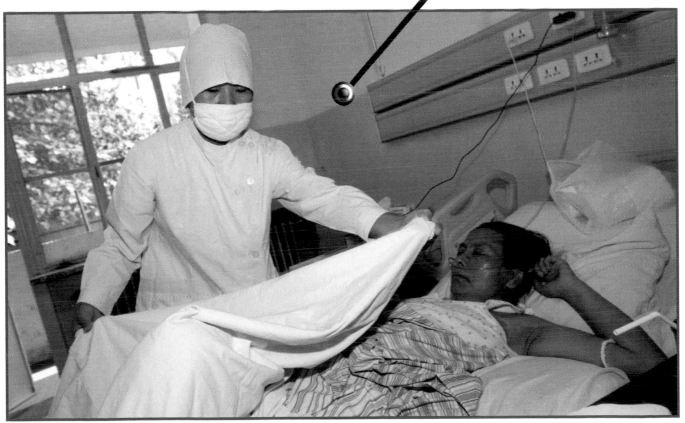

21

Ounce of Prevention

American inventor Benjamin Franklin once said "an ounce of prevention is worth a pound of cure." While some diseases can be treated well with modern medicine, prevention of infection remains the best guarantee of good health.

Wash your hands!

Practicing good hygiene is an easy way to reduce the risk of disease. Although many of the things we touch appear perfectly clean, there may be pathogenic microbes which we cannot see lurking on a doorknob or a dollar. It is important for people to wash their hands often with soap, and to avoid touching their eyes, noses, and mouths after touching dirty surfaces.

In Japan, it is considered polite for a cold sufferer to wear a cloth mask over their nose and mouth when out in public to avoid spreading the virus.

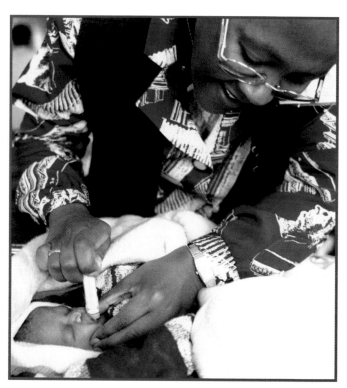

Sanitation is also very important in preventing the spread of disease. Plagues spread quickly without clean drinking water and proper disposal of toilet waste. If household trash is left to pile up in the streets, rotting food will attract pests such as rats, which can also spread disease.

(above) In South Africa, a country suffering from the AIDS pandemic, a baby whose mother is HIV-positive is given a dose of a drug shortly after birth. The drug reduces the chances of HIV being transmitted from mother to child at birth. Unfortunately, the drug is very expensive and not always available.

French scientist Louis Pasteur discovered that viruses that had been killed by exposure to heat or weakened by passage through several animal hosts, provided protection against the disease they caused. This process was called vaccination. English doctor Edward Jenner developed a vaccine against smallpox, a horrible disease unknown today.

Smallpox and cowpox

In the 1700s, a European epidemic of a disease called smallpox led to research on a cure. Smallpox produces sores filled with pus on the skin of its victims as well as fever and blood infections. Thousands died from smallpox outbreaks. The lucky patients who recovered from the disease were left with ugly scars on their faces and bodies.

In 1796, English doctor Edward Jenner noticed that milkmaids who milked cows rarely suffered from smallpox. Milkmaids often caught cowpox, a milder form of the smallpox virus, from the cows they milked. The milkmaid's immune system was exposed to cowpox and produced antibodies that prevented them from getting the disease. Jenner discovered that if he injected a small amount of material from a cowpox lesion, or sore, into a patient and then exposed them to smallpox, they would not be infected. The success of the smallpox **vaccine** has eliminated the disease completely from the earth's population.

Washing your hands with soap and water can help you avoid catching viruses, such as the cold.

After a Plague

A major plague affects more than just the health of a population. By killing large portions of the population, a plague can change the course of history.

The end of the feudal system

In the early 1300s, before the bubonic plague hit many areas of Europe, European society was ruled by the feudal system. Under the feudal system, a small number of nobles, known as lords, owned all of the land and a large number of peasants worked on the land for little pay.

The bubonic plague killed so many people in the mid-1300s that this system was no longer practical. Many landowners and their families died of the plague, leaving no one to **inherit** their land. The deaths of large numbers of peasants also meant that there was a shortage of people to work the land. Skilled tradesmen became rare and valued. Workers could now demand better treatment and higher wages.

A new world order

In the late 1500s, when European explorers ventured across the Atlantic Ocean searching for riches in North and South America, they brought unknown destruction with them. Native Americans had never before been exposed to diseases such as smallpox and **measles**, that had been endemic, or existed in Europe for centuries. Europeans had built up a **resistance** to these plagues, so the diseases were not fatal to them.

Native peoples had no resistance and died in large numbers. This allowed Spanish explorers, or conquistadors, to more easily defeat the Aztecs of Mexico and the Inca of Peru in battle.

Spanish conquistadors brought an end to the great Aztec and Inca empires of North and South America partly through the diseases they brought with them.

Fevers and rebellion

Yellow fever was also brought to North and South America by Europeans. Unlike measles and smallpox, yellow fever was not common in Europe. It was spread to the Caribbean islands when the French army brought in boatloads of slaves taken from Africa, where the disease was endemic. The African slaves were resistant to the disease, but the French army was not. Slaves began to battle against their French masters, who were dying of yellow fever by the dozens. This made it difficult for France to hold on to these territories, since they had to send more and more troops. France was forced to sell a large portion of its territory to the United States government. That land now makes up the state of Louisiana and much of the central United States.

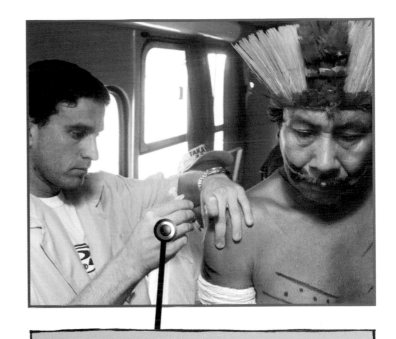

A doctor gives a yellow fever vaccination to a member of the Bacari people of Brazil. With the vaccine, yellow fever kills far fewer people. This man was vaccinated while on his way to a protest against the celebration of Brazil's discovery by Europeans. Many native South Americans died after contact with European diseases they had no immunity to.

Influenza patients lie in a ward at a U.S. Army camp hospital in France, during World War I. The Spanish Flu pandemic of 1918 to 1919 killed more people than all the armies in the war. It was thought that more American soldiers died from the flu than from the fighting during the war.

Living Through Plague

Some plagues end naturally. Others just become endemic to a population. Usually, a pandemic is stopped through the efforts of governments, medical and scientific organizations, and volunteers.

Living through polio

In 1952, a scientist named Jonas Salk discovered a vaccine for poliomyelitis. Dr. Salk and many other researchers studied the disease for years and worked hard to find a cure. Poliomyelitis, or polio, is a disease caused by a virus that attacks the body's nervous system. The nervous system sends messages between the muscles and the brain. The damage caused by polio can stop muscles from functioning, resulting in paralysis, or the inability to move an arm or a leg, or even the muscles in the chest that allow a person to breathe. Polio was a very common disease in the early to mid-1900s. Dr. Salk's work involved examining millions of samples from millions of patients infected with polio. There were three known **strains** of the virus, so the successful vaccine had to contain all three types. Dr. Salk and other researchers examined millions of samples to make sure that only these three forms of the virus could cause polio. Otherwise, a person could be vaccinated, but still die from another unknown type of the disease.

Dr. Jonas Salk with his microscope in the lab at Pittsburgh's Municipal Hospital laboratory. A successful polio vaccine was announced on April 18, 1955.

Tests and more tests

Once a polio vaccine was developed, it was tested on animals. It was then tested on patients already infected with polio, to see if it caused an increase in the number of polio antibodies produced by the immune system. The vaccine was next tested on patients who were not infected with polio, where it also caused an increase in polio antibodies. These volunteers were very brave. Even though the vaccine had already been successfully tested on monkeys, there was still a chance that the vaccine itself could make them sick, or that it would not protect them from the disease.

A young polio victim practices walking with newly-fitted splints.

Living in an "iron lung"

Polio was a frightening disease because it usually affected children and it was very fast-acting. It left many children in wheelchairs, or walking with canes or braces for the rest of their lives. Children would go to bed one night feeling slightly unwell, and wake up the next morning unable to move their legs, or even unable to breathe. Some victims were forced to lie in hospital beds with their chests encased in large machines called iron lungs. Iron lungs expanded and contracted, pushing air in and out of a patient's lungs.

Working together for a cure

It takes a lot of money to search for a cure for a disease. Scientists work for years on projects. Researchers have been hunting for a cure for AIDS since the early 1980s. While some medications have been developed to treat the symptoms of the disease, science is still far from a vaccine or a cure. The research has cost billions of dollars so far. The success of the Salk vaccine shows how ordinary people can work together with scientists to find a cure for a dangerous disease.

(right) Franklin D. Roosevelt later became President of the United States.

Boys raise money to fight polio in the early 1950s. In 1952, more than 57,600 Americans contracted polio. The vaccine was partly funded by penny and dime drives.

The March of Dimes

In 1921, Franklin D. Roosevelt was stricken with polio. He was paralyzed from the waist down, and confined to a wheelchair. Roosevelt began a **non-profit organization** that later became known as the March of Dimes. The March of Dimes raised money to fight polio. It encouraged people to send their dimes to the White House to support polio research. The March of Dimes gave money to fund the work of Dr. Salk, and to test and distribute the polio vaccine. The foundation also provided funding for an oral polio vaccine developed in 1962.

Eliminating the disease

Today, newborn babies in many parts of the world are given the oral polio vaccine. Only six countries in the world still report cases of polio. The disease is close to being eliminated completely, but funding is still needed. Hundreds of millions of dollars a year are required to vaccinate newborn babies worldwide. The Global Polio Eradication Initiative has been established to eliminate the disease by 2008. The initiative joins national governments, health organizations, and private charities such as the Rotary Club, to bring an end to polio.

Funding a cure for AIDS

The search for a polio vaccine is an example of how scientists, governments, and volunteer groups worked together to find a cure for a disease. That example is being followed in the search for a cure for HIV/AIDS. Drug companies have developed many treatments for Human Immunodeficiency Virus (HIV) that have improved the health and lengthened the lives of people who have the virus. So far, researchers have not had any luck in their search for a cure. They are still working on an AIDS vaccine. A vaccine could take decades and billions of dollars to develop but it would save many lives. AIDS has killed millions of people in the past 20 years. It has devastated parts of southern Africa, where two thirds of all HIV/AIDS cases are reported. More than ten million African children have been orphaned by AIDS and often their governments cannot care for them. AIDS experts believe the pandemic will get worse in Africa, Asia, and parts of eastern Europe in the coming years.

Many organizations raise funds to fight AIDS, but it is not always easy. These people are marching to ask governments to help in the fight against AIDS.

Disease Trail

Cholera is a disease caused by bacteria in drinking water contaminated by human waste. In 1854, Dr. John Snow discovered the cause of cholera by tracing the spread of an outbreak.

People in the Broad Street and Golden Square area of London, England, began to fall ill with cholera. Five hundred people died in ten days.

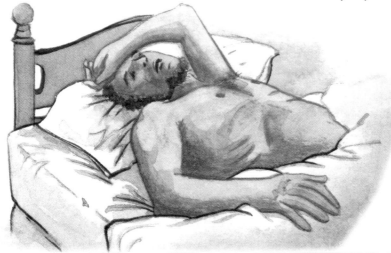

Dr. John Snow, who had been studying cholera since the early 1830s, became interested in the outbreak.

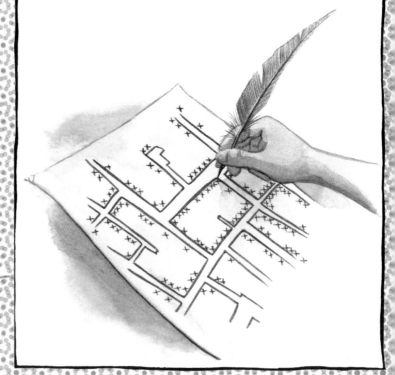

Using a map of the area, Dr. Snow marked off the location of each victim's home.

Next, Dr. Snow tried to relate the location of the victims to the source of their drinking water. He found that they all drank from the same water pump on Broad Street.

Dr. Snow examined the well and found that it was being contaminated by drainage from toilets and sinks.

Dr. Snow convinced city officials to remove the handle from the water pump, and no new cases of cholera were found in the neighborhood.

Glossary

agency A business or service that acts for others

antibody A substance produced by the body to destroy or weaken disease-causing bacteria and make the body immune to the disease

antigen A substance that helps produce antibodies when introduced into the body

bacteria (bacterium) A group of organisms, some of which cause disease

climate The normal weather conditions of an area

devastating Terrible or destroying

host The animal or plant on which another organism lives

immune system A body system of organs, tissues, cells, and other parts that recognizes and fights diseases when they enter the body

infection Invasion by disease-causing bacteria in a body part

infectious diseases Diseases that can be passed from person to person

inherit Something passed down from a parent

measles A disease with fever and red skin spots that usually happens in childhood

microbes Tiny life forms or microorganisms that cause disease

microscope An instrument that magnifies objects too small to be seen by the eye

molecule The smallest bit or particle of something

non-profit organization An agency that performs a function but does not make money from it

phlegm Thick, sticky mucus

pus A yellowish fluid formed in infections

religious pilgrims People who travel to and from holy or religious places

resistance The ability to defend against disease

strain Things that come from the same group or kind

suffocated To cut off air or breathing

tissue A group of cells from a specific part of the body

United Nations An international organization that promotes peace, security, and health

vaccine A preparation given to bring on immunity against a disease

viruses Very tiny infectious organisms that cause illness

white blood cells Cells contained in blood that fight disease

Index

1 2 3 4 5 6 7 8 9 0 Printed in the U.S.A. 3 2 1 0 9 8 7 6 5 4